YOU KNOW YOU ARE

GETTING OLDER...

by Richard McChesney

illustrated by Brighty

You Know You Are Getting Older... will cheer up anyone who is frustrated with the ageing process. They say laughter is the best medicine!

This is the sixth book in the "You Know You Are" book series and with 40 illustrated captions, you can't help but see the humorous side of ageing.

Other books in the "You Know You Are" series are:

- You Know You Are A Runner...
- You Know You Are A Nurse...
- You Know You Are An Engineer...
- You Know You Are A Dog Lover...
- You Know You Are A Golfer...
- You Know You Are A Teacher...
- You Know You Are A Mother...

Visit www.YouKnowYouAreBooks.com to join our mailing list and be notified when future titles are released, or find us at www.facebook.com/YouKnowYouAreBooks, or follow us on twitter (@YouKnowYouAreBK)

STRICTLY
BUSINESS

YOU KNOW YOU ARE GETTING OLDER
WHEN YOU SMILE ALL THE TIME BECAUSE YOU
CAN'T HEAR A THING ANYONE IS SAYING...

YOU KNOW YOU ARE GETTING OLDER
WHEN YOU'RE HAVING A PARTY AND
THE NEIGHBORS DON'T REALIZE IT...

YOU KNOW YOU ARE GETTING OLDER
WHEN YOUR EARS ARE HAIRIER
THAN YOUR HEAD...

YOU KNOW YOU ARE GETTING OLDER
WHEN YOU NO LONGER THINK OF THE SPEED LIMIT AS A CHALLENGE...

YOU KNOW YOU ARE GETTING OLDER
WHEN YOUR CHILDREN EARN SALARIES, NOT ALLOWANCES...

YOU KNOW YOU ARE GETTING OLDER
WHEN YOU STILL OWN A
RECORD COLLECTION...

YOU KNOW YOU ARE GETTING OLDER
WHEN YOU STILL WISH YOUR PARENTS WOULD
BUY YOU THAT BIKE WITH THE BANANA SEAT
AND U-SHAPED HANDLE BARS...

YOU KNOW YOU ARE GETTING OLDER
WHEN YOU STILL LOOK FOR THE
TOY IN YOUR CEREAL BOX...

YOU KNOW YOU ARE GETTING OLDER
WHEN YOU DON'T CARE WHERE YOUR
SPOUSE GOES AS LONG AS YOU
DON'T HAVE TO GO TOO...

YOU KNOW YOU ARE GETTING OLDER

WHEN YOU ARE TOLD TO SLOW DOWN BY YOUR DOCTOR INSTEAD OF THE POLICE...

YOU KNOW YOU ARE GETTING OLDER
WHEN 'GETTING LUCKY' MEANS LOCATING
YOUR CAR IN THE PARKING LOT...

YOU KNOW YOU ARE GETTING OLDER
WHEN YOU WAKE UP WITH A HANGOVER BUT YOU DIDN'T DRINK THE NIGHT BEFORE...

YOU KNOW YOU ARE GETTING OLDER
WHEN 6AM IS THE TIME YOU WAKE UP,
NOT WHEN YOU GO TO BED...

YOU KNOW YOU ARE GETTING OLDER
WHEN AN 'ALL NIGHTER' MEANS
NOT GETTING UP TO PEE...

YOU KNOW YOU ARE GETTING OLDER WHEN DINNER AND A MOVIE IS THE WHOLE DATE, RATHER THAN THE START OF ONE...

YOU KNOW YOU ARE GETTING OLDER
WHEN YOUR CO-WORKERS WERE
BORN AROUND THE SAME YEAR
YOU GOT YOUR LAST PROMOTION...

YOU KNOW YOU ARE GETTING OLDER
WHEN THE LITTLE GREY-HAIRED LADY YOU
HELP ACROSS THE STREET IS YOUR WIFE...

YOU KNOW YOU ARE GETTING OLDER
WHEN THE PHARMACIST HAS BECOME YOUR NEW BEST FRIEND...

YOU KNOW YOU ARE GETTING OLDER
WHEN YOU REMEMBER THE DAYS OF
WOODEN SCHOOL DESKS...

YOU KNOW YOU ARE GETTING OLDER

WHEN YOU REMEMBER A TIME WHEN 'GAY' MEANT JOYOUS AND LIVELY, MERRY, HAPPY, LIGHT-HEARTED...

YOU KNOW YOU ARE GETTING OLDER
WHEN YOU GET THE SAME SENSATION
FROM A ROCKING CHAIR THAT YOU
ONCE GOT FROM A ROLLER COASTER...

YOU KNOW YOU ARE GETTING OLDER
WHEN YOU KNOW ALL THE ANSWERS BUT
NOBODY ASKS YOU THE QUESTIONS...

YOU KNOW YOU ARE GETTING OLDER
WHEN YOU DISCOVER WHERE YOUR PROSTRATE IS...

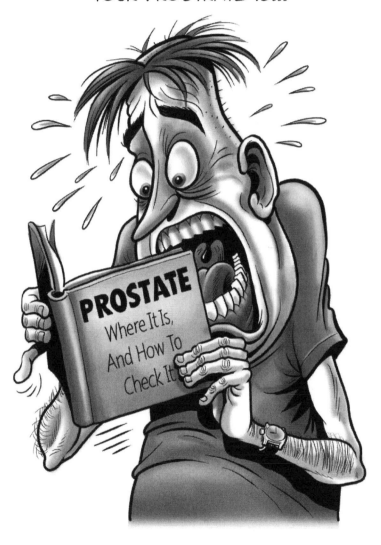

YOU KNOW YOU ARE GETTING OLDER
WHEN YOU LOOK FOR YOUR GLASSES FOR
HALF AN HOUR, AND THEY WERE ON
YOUR HEAD THE WHOLE TIME...

YOU KNOW YOU ARE GETTING OLDER
WHEN YOU LOOK FORWARD TO A DULL EVENING...

YOU KNOW YOU ARE GETTING OLDER
WHEN YOUR ROCK-HARD ABS HAVE TURNED TO PILLOW-SOFT FLABS...

YOU KNOW YOU ARE GETTING OLDER
WHEN YOU TALK ABOUT 'GOOD GRASS' AND
YOU ARE REFERRING TO SOMEONE'S LAWN...

YOU KNOW YOU ARE GETTING OLDER

WHEN TURNING OUT THE LIGHTS IS MORE
ABOUT SAVING MONEY THAN ROMANCE...

YOU KNOW YOU ARE GETTING OLDER
WHEN YOUR IDEA OF WEIGHTLIFTING IS STANDING UP...

YOU KNOW YOU ARE GETTING OLDER
WHEN YOUR SATURDAY NIGHT FEVER TURNS
INTO SATURDAY NIGHT HOT FLASHES...

YOU KNOW YOU ARE GETTING OLDER

WHEN CANDLELIT DINNERS ARE NO LONGER ROMANTIC BECAUSE YOU CAN'T READ THE MENU...

YOU KNOW YOU ARE GETTING OLDER
WHEN YOU GET THE URGE, BUT YOU CAN'T REMEMBER WHAT FOR...

YOU KNOW YOU ARE GETTING OLDER
WHEN THINGS YOU BUY NOW WON'T WEAR OUT...

YOU KNOW YOU ARE GETTING OLDER
WHEN THE TWINKLE IN YOUR EYE
IS JUST THE REFLECTION OF
THE SUN ON YOUR BIFOCALS...

YOU KNOW YOU ARE GETTING OLDER
WHEN YOUR JOINTS CAN PREDICT WEATHER
PATTERNS BETTER THAN THE EXPERTS...

So... are you

Getting Older?

You have just read the sixth book in the "You Know You Are" series.

Other "You Know You Are" books are:

- You Know You Are A Runner...
- You Know You Are A Nurse...
- You Know You Are An Engineer...
- You Know You Are A Dog Lover...
- You Know You Are A Golfer...
- You Know You Are A Teacher...
- You Know You Are A Mother...

If you enjoyed this book why not join our mailing list to be notified when future titles are released – visit www.YouKnowYouAreBooks.com, or find us on facebook (www.facebook.com/YouKnowYouAreBooks), or follow us on twitter (@YouKnowYouAreBK)

Other 'You Know You Are' books include:

Visit www.YouKnowYouAreBooks.com for further details.

Printed in Great Britain
by Amazon